D0262165

a guide to

crystals

a guide to

crystals

Jennie Harding

This is a Parragon Book

First published in 2002

Parragon

Queen Street House

4 Queen Street

Bath BA1 1HE, UK

Copyright © Parragon 2002

All rights reserved. No part of this publication may be reproduced,
stored in a retrieval system or transmitted, in any form or by any means,
electronic, mechanical, photocopying, recording or otherwise, without
the prior permission of the copyright holder.

ISBN: 0–75257–778–6

Printed in China.

Produced by the Bridgewater Book Company Ltd.

NOTE

Any information given in this book is not intended to be taken
as a replacement for medical advice. Any person with a condition requiring
medical attention should consult a qualified medical practitioner or therapist.

DEDICATION

This book is dedicated with love to my mother Sonja, who takes such care
of all the stones and crystals in her beautiful collection.

ACKNOWLEDGEMENTS

The publishers wish to thank the following for the use of pictures:
Corbis UK Ltd: 6t, 7t, 22, 25b, 27t, 28t, 30b, 32t, 36b, 37b, 52t; *Crown Copyright:
Historic Royal Palaces, Hampton Court*: 13t; *Getty Images*: 8b, 12t, 16t, 24b, 42b,
44b, 50b, 53b; *Hulton Getty*: 14; 39b, 41t, 51t; *International Colored Gemstone
Association (ICA) (www.gemstone.org)*: 39t, 41b; *Kobal Collection*: 15t;
NASA: 59b; *PA News Photos*: 12b; *Rex Diamond Mining Corporation
(www.rexmining.com)*: 11t; *Science Photo Library*: 9t, 27b, 31t, 43b, 61b.

contents

Introduction

The amazing world of crystals and jewels never ceases to fascinate us. Even in our everyday language we talk about a brilliant idea being 'a gem', or about things being 'as clear as crystal'. Ask anyone what is the most valuable thing they can think of and many will answer 'diamonds' – didn't Marilyn Monroe claim they were 'a girl's best friend'?

An engagement ring containing a diamond or other gems is given as a symbol of something rare and precious that will last for ever. At the heart of our deep and long-lasting regard for these valuable and beautiful glittering gifts of the Earth is the idea that they are eternally special.

Engagement rings containing diamonds are a symbol of eternal and enduring love.

Fortunately, as well as precious stones, there are crystals like quartz, amethyst, moonstone or garnet, which are also beautiful and much more affordable, either as jewellery, stones for a collection or for healing purposes. This book will explore all of these aspects, especially the use of stones as tools for balancing the energies of body, mind and spirit. This is a practice with deep historical roots; many stones have ancient associations with different physical or mental conditions. In India to this very day, gems are ground to a powder and mixed with water, then drunk for their healing properties, just as they were hundreds of years ago. In the Crystal Index, found in the middle of this book on pages 21–53, we shall link thirty-two minerals and stones to their different colours and learn their

Quartz crystals can be used as healing tools to balance the energy of the body.

The brilliant lustre of diamonds endeared them to Marilyn Monroe's character Lorelei Lee in Gentlemen Prefer Blondes.

the information given on particular stones will help you to realise why.

Bringing crystals into your personal space is a way of creating a connection with the Earth, since all crystals are born and grow within our planet's structure. If you use them with care and respect, crystals will share with you the positive energy of their light, colour and beauty. Whether you simply collect or wear them or use them to enhance your energy, crystals are a source of wonder. Enjoy this crystal journey through the worlds of geology, history, legend and healing.

The vibrant purple hues of an amethyst crystal have a soothing effect on the mind.

geological characteristics, as well as their history and healing uses.

Crystals can be used to beautify and clear the energies of your environment, as tools for meditation and contemplation, and of course can also be worn on your person. Perhaps the wearing of jewellery will take on a different meaning when you discover some of the fascinating geological and historical facts about the stones. You may find that you have already instinctively brought crystals into your environment and

Mother Earth: Planet of Rebirth

Our story starts with the creation of the Earth – with the origin of minerals in the very structure of the planet on which we live. Minerals are natural, inorganic chemical substances. Approximately 2500 different types exist.

The mineral kingdom provides the chemical building blocks for everything on the Earth: rocks, plants, animals – and humans. About 90 per cent of each of us is made of water, and the rest is minerals!

The Earth is Always Moving

The Earth originally formed out of clouds of gas and the dust of other stars. Heavy elements like nickel and iron sank to form the hot core, which is still molten, made of liquid

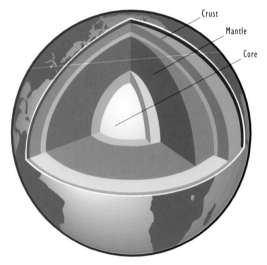

The Earth is made up of different layers. These are liquid at the core and solid on the surface.

Crust

Mantle

Core

minerals that are slowly pushed up to the surface. Lighter minerals such as silicon and oxygen, the ingredients of quartz, form part of a thicker, sometimes semi-molten layer called the mantle. Finally, the very lightest minerals float up to the surface of the Earth. This part, which is where we live and walk, is called the crust. Earthquake zones or volcanic areas like

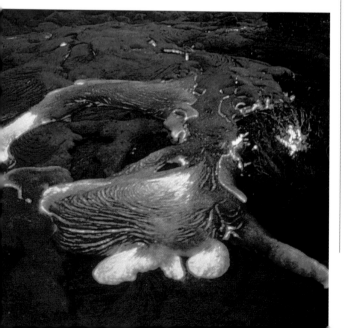

Flowing red-hot lava spills onto the Earth's surface after a volcanic eruption.

The Three Main Types of Rocks

Igneous: these layers originally formed as a mass of molten rock (called magma) deep inside the Earth's core. They rise to cover the crust through cracks or volcanic eruptions. Combined with water in the upper layers just below the surface, magma may form quartz crystals in large gaps called veins. Depending on the other minerals present, gems like emeralds or aquamarine may form.

Metamorphic: these are rock layers that have been changed after their original formation, usually by increases in pressure, heat, water vapour or chemical reactions. For example, layers of clay and sand sinking into the crust under pressure can form the mineral compound corundum, otherwise known as sapphire or ruby.

Sedimentary: these are layers of soft rock on the surface, formed by the actions of wind and water on surface minerals. The most common is limestone.

Rubies are one of the most precious gems that can be found in the world.

Mount Etna in Sicily show how thin the crust actually is. As heat from the Earth's core pushes minerals upwards, cooler rocks sink, melt at the core and are pushed up to the surface again. The Earth is constantly shifting and recycling minerals.

The Earth's Floating Crust

The Earth's crust literally floats on the mantle. It is made up of different sections or 'plates'; wherever these collide with each other, the pressure folds rocks into mountains or bursts open volcanoes. Deep in the oceans, cracks in the crust allow new mineral masses to grow, pushing continents sideways. This movement happens because of the cycles of rising heated minerals and sinking cooler layers. New sources of precious stones and gems continue to be found because the Earth's surface is never static, and the location of stones and gems is always changing. Even though this process takes millions of years, new mineral layers are continually being formed within the Earth's structure.

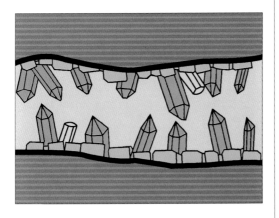

Crystals form in pockets or areas of space between rock layers. Mining techniques have developed to harvest these treasures.

The Making of Crystals

The many compounds of minerals that are found in the Earth's crust have been classified into different groups. Here are some of the most significant categories, which include many of the stones that you are likely to encounter.

Crystal Shapes and Inclusions

A crystal is a chemical compound that has changed naturally from a liquid to a solid with a regular geometric form and smooth sides. Crystals follow geometrical principles as their molecules arrange themselves. Quartz crystals divide and subdivide themselves along a hexagonal axis, meaning they typically have six sides called 'faces'. The points are called 'terminations' and crystals with points at both ends are 'double terminated'. It is also possible for twin crystals to form like mirror images of each other. Some crystals contain specks that look like flaws, but which are simply air bubbles or specks of other minerals; these are called 'inclusions'. Rutilated quartz contains many hairlike strands of rutile, a mineral sometimes called 'Venus' hair'.

Crystals are mined from deep inside the Earth's crust. This is not a modern phenomenon – mining has been carried out for centuries.

Clear quartz crystals make good healing wands because of their shape.

Crystal Extraction Methods

In ancient times, our ancestors gathered crystals from the surface of the Earth quite spontaneously, and even today mineral enthusiasts still do this. Mining for metals and crystals has been happening since the Stone Age, with very well established workings in the Middle East during Roman times. Modern industrial mining for many kinds of precious stones takes place extensively in countries such as Sri Lanka, Brazil and South Africa. When you buy a crystal it is worth remembering it has come via the miner, the wholesaler, the retailer and others before reaching you. This is why cleansing the crystals you buy is so important (see pages 20–21).

Amber is fossilised tree resin, which is millions of years old.

Pearls are another example of an organic material. In this case, the origin is animal.

Organic Minerals

'Organic' in this context means something with plant or animal origins. A few such minerals exist. Amber, for example, is the fossilised resin of an ancient pine tree. Pearls form when a grain of sand irritates the inner lining of the pearl oyster.

Main Groups of Metals and Crystals

Native elements (*uncombined with other elements*) gold, silver, platinum, copper, carbon (as diamond).

Sulphides (*metal plus sulphur*) iron plus sulphur makes pyrite (fool's gold).

Oxides (*main group is silicon dioxide, making quartz*) clear quartz, amethyst, rose quartz, smoky quartz; also microcrystalline forms called chalcedony, the name given to crystals such as carnelian and tiger's eye because of their waxy or translucent appearance. Opals are similar to quartz but are made of silicon dioxide and water. Aluminium oxide forms the compound corundum, whose red and blue forms are rubies and sapphires respectively.

Silicates within this group are feldspars comprising a huge number of crystals, very common in the Earth's crust. Moonstone and labradorite are varieties of feldspar made up of sodium and calcium. Another large silicate group are garnets, which may be rich in aluminium, iron or chromium depending on their location. Other silicate minerals are tourmaline and the beryls, including aquamarine and emerald.

Royal Crystals

Crystals and precious stones have long been valued as hunting tools, carvings, jewellery or icons. They were used as badges of royalty and power, symbolising the unique status of kings and queens. They are so precious that wars have been fought over them.

The Ancient Egyptians were mining emeralds, peridot, lapis lazuli and other precious stones over 3000 years ago. They were highly skilled in polishing and setting in gold and their work can still be admired in their relics, especially the treasures of the Pharaohs. For thousands of years, diamonds and other gems have been mined in India, Sri Lanka and Burma (now called Myanmar), as well as countries in South America and Africa. The ancient Mayan and Chinese civilisations produced exquisite carvings of jade and emerald.

Queen Elizabeth II wearing the Imperial State Crown, one of the most important items of regalia in the Crown Jewels.

The Tower of London, surrounded by the famous ravens, is where the British Crown Jewels can be seen.

The British Royal Family's Crown Jewels

The Jewel House in the Tower of London contains all of the British Royal Family's regalia. The most famous element of this collection is St Edward's Crown, which is worn by the reigning monarch. The first Crown Jewels were assembled by King Edward the Confessor in the eleventh century. In

The History of the Koh-i-noor

The Koh-i-noor, one of the largest diamonds in the world, is set in the crown of Queen Elizabeth the Queen Mother.

The Koh-i-noor is one of the largest single diamonds in the world and was first owned by the Rajah of Malwa in India in 1304. It has a weight of 186 carats. To put this weight into perspective, most modern diamond engagement rings weigh approximately 0.25 to 1 carat. For several hundred years, the jewel belonged to various Indian emperors. In 1739, the Shah of Persia invaded Delhi and pillaged the city to find the legendary diamond. He was told that the defeated emperor had the jewel hidden in his turban. He invited his captive to exchange turbans. Unrolling the cloth the Shah found the jewel. He cried out 'Koh-i-noor!', or 'Mountain of light!' – which remained its name.

When Lahore, the capital of Punjab, was annexed to British India in 1849, the stone passed to the East India Company, who presented it to Queen Victoria in 1850. It was displayed at the Crystal Palace exhibition, disappointing viewers because it did not appear to sparkle enough. Queen Victoria therefore had the diamond re-cut, reducing it from 186 carats to 108.93.

In 1911 the stone was set in the crown of Queen Mary. In 1937 the diamond was reset, this time in the crown of Queen Elizabeth the Queen Mother.

1216, King John Plantagenet subsequently lost them in quicksand in East Anglia. The next collection also had a rather chequered history. During the Civil War in 1649, Oliver Cromwell ordered them to be broken up; however, remnants were saved and later incorporated into the new regalia fashioned for King Charles II when he ascended the throne in 1661. Today, the collection is priceless. In the early twentieth century, the largest diamond ever found, the Cullinan, was cut into four segments. One segment, known as the 'Star of Africa', is carried in the Sovereign's Sceptre. It weighs more than 530 carats and has 74 facets, making it the world's largest cut diamond.

Crystals Today

In the early twentieth century, fabulous jewels began to adorn famous Hollywood movie stars and be seen regularly on the screen and in magazines. It is not surprising that these legendary bejewelled icons have become as admired as royalty.

Famous Women and their Gems

The screen goddess Marlene Dietrich loved emeralds, especially those carved into smooth-domed cabochons. She once lost a 37-carat emerald ring in a cake mixture and found it again in a piece of the cake! Elizabeth Taylor has been one of Hollywood's greatest stars, with an amazing jewellery collection. The Taylor–Burton diamond given to her by Richard Burton weighs almost 70 carats. She also has a collection of dazzling emerald jewellery that once belonged to a Russian Grand Duchess. Jacqueline Kennedy Onassis also collected dazzling pieces, especially from her second husband Aristotle Onassis. His engagement ring to her was auctioned at Sotheby's for $2.6 million in 1996. When Princess Diana's fine sparkling sapphire and diamond engagement ring was originally shown to the world's press, it sparked a fashion for copies of the design.

Marlene Dietrich, the legendary screen icon, adored emeralds, especially when they were cut into smooth, rounded cabochons.

In the film Diamonds are Forever, *James Bond discovers the power of diamonds and what others will do to get them.*

Crystal Movies

Even in our sophisticated age, nothing beats a good adventure story, as film-makers know very well. The idea of a dangerous hunt for a huge, priceless emerald inspired the film *Romancing the Stone*, and the James Bond epic *Diamonds are Forever*, as well known for the song as for the story, deals with diamonds as a source of staggering wealth and power. In the 1970s and early 1980s, the 'Superman' movies introduced new ideas: namely that crystals could hold energy and even power spacecraft! It also explored the idea that diamonds could hold information – an idea realised in the development of the silicon chip. This interesting shift in presentation coincided with a general interest in crystals for healing.

The New Age – Expanding Crystal Awareness

Since the 1960s, crystals have been used increasingly as healing tools. Many writers have linked this awareness to the New Age, a rise in spiritual consciousness, particularly towards the dawn of the New Millennium. In fact, crystals have been used for healing since before Egyptian times. However, with advances in geology and quantum physics, the structure and energy of crystals is beginning to be understood in different terms. People are made up of the same elements as crystals. We are made of the same minerals that are recycled by the Earth in spite of the fact that we are organic beings, and minerals are inorganic. Perhaps one way of explaining the response to crystal energies is to say we subtly recognise elements that are in us all.

A rose quartz crystal placed on the body can enhance relaxation and feelings of wellbeing and happiness.

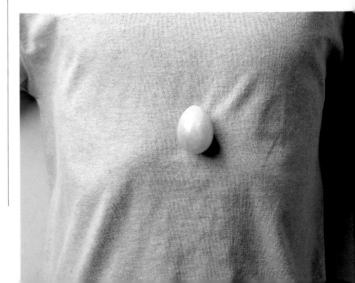

Crystals, Colours and Chakras

One of the most striking things about crystals is their colour. This is often what first attracts us, such as when our eye is drawn to the vivid green of emeralds or the deep purple of amethysts. Different colours can affect us physically and emotionally – for example, the blue green of the sea is calming to the eyes and the spirit.

The colour spectrum can be used as a model for understanding the different energies at work in our bodies.

Colour Healing

If you take a cut-glass pendulum and hang it in a sunny window, your walls will be covered in many dancing rainbows showing the seven pure colour shades of the spectrum – red, orange, yellow, green, blue, indigo and violet. The white light that splits into all these colours is the only part of the spectrum we can see, although insects and some animals can see infrared and ultraviolet waves too.

In ancient Egyptian times, healers chose ingredients for their patients on the basis of the colour of the problem. For example, red was for blood, purple for bruising, yellow for jaundice. The wearing of

The rainbow colours to be found in crystals show all the colours of the spectrum. Specific colours are used in different healing methods.

When we see blue or green shades, in nature or elsewhere, these act as a relaxant and have a calming effect on us.

clothes or jewellery of that colour came to be associated with the prevention of the condition; if you had poor circulation you were advised to wear red. (This is because cold feet do become warmer more quickly in red socks than in any other colour.)

By the twentieth century, scientists were beginning to experiment with light waves, noting that the properties of the red and orange rays were 'warmer', and the blue and purple rays 'cooler', with the colour green in the middle as a balance. These days, light frequencies directed through lasers are being used in surgery and for healing wounded tissue.

The Chakra System

Several thousand years ago, in India, the energy frequencies of the body were perceived as being on seven different levels, each corresponding to an area in the body, centred in a 'chakra' or 'wheel'. The white light of universal energy was considered to enter through the crown of the head and then modulated in frequency through each of the colour levels from violet at the crown to red at the base of the spine. This ancient model is widely used in healing work and yoga practice today.

Meditating on the colours of the rainbow can bring strong feelings of relaxation and calm.

Chakra	Colour	Gland	Body Area
crown	violet	pineal	top of head
third eye	indigo	pituitary	mid-forehead
throat	blue	thyroid	throat
heart	green	thymus	centre of chest
solar plexus	yellow	spleen	under diaphragm
sacrum	orange	ovaries/testes	lower abdomen
root	red	adrenals	base of spine

Within each colour, shades are possible. Green can vary from yellow-green to emerald to dark green, but all shades relate to the heart chakra.

Small crystals can easily be placed on your body and around your living and working environment.

The way universal energy passes into the body is though the breath. As you breathe in—not just air but life force—the energy levels are maintained at appropriate levels. However, if there is disharmony, then other help may be needed. Colors and crystals can be used to rebalance diminished chakra energies.

Color Healing Chart

This color healing chart is designed to suggest links between colors, body energies, color effects, chakra centers, and crystals. The original seven colors of the spectrum have been expanded to include shades, as well as rays like silver. This chart corresponds exactly with the Crystal Index (pages 22–53), where individual stones are discussed in detail. Guided by the way you feel, you will be able to choose the appropriate colors to help you, as well as select useful crystals. You will find some simple crystal healing methods described on pages 54–55.

Some of these correspondences may be surprising. Black, for example, often has an undeserved negative association, but it can

have quite a different meaning. In many healing traditions such as that of the Native Americans, for example, black is simply seen as the complement to white. Observing the night sky, the darkness creates the shadow that lets the light of the stars appear like diamonds on black velvet. Native American teachings revere the darkness as the source of mystery, the place from which all new things are born. Every creation myth on Earth relates the origin of the planet to a time of dark formlessness, out of which came light.

Here are some examples showing how you can use the chart. If you feel cold and lacking in energy, you will see that red is a warming color and garnets are suggested. You can either find some red in your wardrobe, or try wearing the crystal or meditating on it (see pages 58–59). If you are afraid of change, try wearing or meditating with labradorite. If you want to expand a relationship, wear amber colors or the stone. You will discover your own favorite colors and stones very quickly. If you find yourself using a lot of one particular stone or color, then that chakra clearly needs energizing.

Tumblestones are examples of small polished crystals that are very easy to __ carry around with you.

The Colour Healing Chart

Colour	Energy	Effect	Chakra	Stone	
Red	action	warming	root	garnet	
Orange	relationship	expanding	sacrum	amber	
Yellow	mental alertness	clearing	solar plexus	topaz	
Light Green	spontaneity	refreshing	heart	peridot	
Rich Green	love	harmonising	heart	emerald	
Turquoise*	protection	strengthening	heart/thymus	turquoise	
Pale Blue	communication	soothing	throat	celestite	
Dark Blue	intuition	connecting	third eye	lapis lazuli	
Violet	insight	inspiring	crown	amethyst	
Pink	unconditional love	releasing	heart	rose quartz	
White	universal energy	healing	all chakras	clear quartz	
Black	universal mystery	visioning	root	obsidian	
Brown	rootedness	grounding	root	smoky quartz	
Iridescent	change	flowing	third eye	labradorite	
Gold	self-worth	revitalising	crown	gold	
Silver	inner knowledge	calming	third eye	silver	

* Turquoise (blue-green) is often seen as corresponding to a minor chakra point, at the thymus gland in the upper chest, which supports the immune system.

Choosing and Caring for Crystals

Selecting the crystals you want and taking care of them is an important part of building a collection. This can become a very rewarding pastime as well as having interesting subtle effects on you and your living space.

Choosing Crystals

You will be attracted to stones because of their colour, their shape or size, or even for more subtle reasons. Remember, we have discussed that you and crystals share mineral elements in common. Crystals have their own 'frequency' thanks to the arrangement of their

To clean crystals and get rid of any negative energy that might be lingering, hold them under clear running water.

molecules – and so do you. This means that if a crystal jumps out at you or you feel sensations of tingling when you pick up a particular stone, then this is the one for you. It has been demonstrated with willing subjects that human electromagnetic energies change when crystals are brought near the body; you are simply reacting to the stone. Trust that feeling and go with it. (I just hope you are not like me: I always seem to go for the most expensive ones!) Remember there is a difference between a naturally terminated crystal point like quartz and a stone that has been polished, cut or shaped. One is in a natural state and the other has been worked by human hands. They are equally beautiful, but have different energies.

Cleansing Crystals

Having purchased your crystals, it makes sense to clean them. They have been mined, extracted, possibly tumbled or cut, sold to a wholesaler, transported, brought to sale and

If you sit quietly and hold your crystal in your hands, you can 'programme' it with positive energy.

'Programming' Crystals

Programming a crystal means allowing new energy to flow into the crystal from you, making it uniquely yours. You could choose to charge it with the pink ray of unconditional love or visualise pure white universal light flowing down your arms, into your hands and filling the crystal. You can then ask the stone to continue to reflect that love in your personal space, and place it carefully wherever you think it needs to sit.

The Crystal Index

handled by many people before you. Cleansing is not just about removing dirt, grease and dust, it also clears previous energies from the stone. Simply hold your crystal under flowing cold water for several minutes and visualise all other energy traces being dissolved. If you are not sure if the crystal is fully clear, ask in your mind and intuit the response, and repeat until you feel the stone is clear. Crystals should be cleaned regularly, especially if they are used for healing.

The Crystal Index covers the next thirty-two pages. You will find the stones arranged by colour, corresponding to the chart on page 19. The colour ray is further explained, and then each stone is given a profile showing geological, geographical, historical and healing information. As well as reading them all, try flipping the pages and stopping at a colour that attracts you on a particular day. You may need that energy!

Amethyst reflects the colour violet and brings inspiration into our hearts and minds. It is a very popular crystal for healing work.

Red

Red is the bright stimulating colour of action. Wearing red is very energising, and red gemstones help you feel dynamic and confident.

Ruby

Geology: Ruby is a variety of corundum, the second hardest known mineral, coloured red by the element chromium. The most precious rubies can be rarer and more valuable than diamonds. Fine rubies glow like red-hot coals. Pinkish or darker red examples also occur. Some very rare stones show a six-pointed star effect in bright light due to bands of rutile in their structure. These are called star rubies.

Exquisitely carved rubies have been used as personal signet rings to seal documents for centuries.

Sources: In Myanmar, some ruby mines date from the Stone and Bronze Ages. Today this country is still the most famous source of rubies. Thailand produces rubies of a darker colour and is the most important ruby trading centre in the world.

History: 'Ruby' comes from the Latin word *ruber* meaning red. Similar words are found in Persian and Sanskrit for both the stone and the colour red. Rubies have been venerated for thousands of years. In the Old Testament,

God places this 'lord of gems' on Aaron's neck. The Bible also states that wisdom is 'more precious than rubies'.

Healing uses: Ruby lights a fire of courage within you, encouraging you to step beyond yourself to new possibilities. It increases your physical vitality and your physical energy, boosting your circulation and bringing strength to you. It is a stone that symbolises power, leadership and integrity.

Garnet

Geology: Garnets form in igneous and metamorphic rocks under high pressure, and occur in very precise symmetrical crystals with twelve diamond-shaped facets. They are mostly known for their deep red colour, but can be found in pink, orange and even green shades. Pyrope garnets have a dark ruby-red colour, and rhodolite garnets are also popular, with a pinkish to purplish red sheen.

The rich red hues of garnets mean that the stones make very attractive jewellery.

Sources: Pyrope garnets are mined in South Africa and also the USA, specifically in Utah and Arizona, where the common name for them is 'anthill garnets'. This is because tiny examples are excavated by ants when building their nests. The rhodolite variety are obtained from Africa, India and Sri Lanka.

The gleaming seeds of the pomegranate fruit resemble clusters of garnet crystals.

History: The name 'garnet' derives from the pomegranate, a fruit with dark seeds in bright red flesh resembling garnet clusters! Legend has it that Noah's Ark was lit up at night by a garnet lantern, and garnets have traditionally been used as a protective talisman when travelling.

Healing uses: Garnet provides a calm, grounding strength to the physical body. It helps you feel centred with a reservoir of inner strength and confidence. It is used to strengthen and regenerate the body, boosting the circulation and the reproductive energies.

Garnets can be quite large stones and look particularly beautiful when they are set in simple silver or gold.

Warning

Wearing red stones is not recommended for people with high blood pressure or heart problems.

Orange

Warm sunny shades of orange are very positive colours. Orange removes fear and replaces it with optimism, improving your relationships with others.

Amber

Geology: Amber is fossilised resin or tree sap from the ancient pine tree *Pinus succinifera* and has taken approximately 25–50 million years to harden. Amber is also called succinite. Thousands of samples have been found containing whole insects, pollen grains and ancient plants. Amber is organic because of its plant origin. It is usually found in yellow, gold or orange shades, but red, brown and green varieties also exist.

Amber has been worn as an ornament for thousands of years.

Sources: Fine amber is mainly found in the Baltic states and the Dominican Republic.

History: Archaeological finds reveal that humankind has used and revered amber since the Stone Age. In ancient Greece, amber was considered to be the juice or essence of the setting sun. In the epic poem the *Odyssey*, Homer mentions amber being given as a princely gift. In Roman times, amber artefacts were regarded as being more valuable than slaves.

Healing uses: Amber helps lift your spirits. It builds your physical vitality and positively charges your energy levels. It shields you from negativity from other people or from your environment. It is used to clear and rebalance the heart, the abdomen and lower back areas.

Some examples of amber contain whole insects preserved within them. These make interesting pieces of jewellery.

Carnelian

Geology: Carnelian is a variety of chalcedony, a kind of quartz made up of tiny finely grained microcrystals. It is found in shades of apricot, deep orange and even red-brown, and good quality stones have a translucent sheen. It is easily carved and has often been used for seals or signet rings.

Sources: Carnelian comes from Brazil, Uruguay and also from India. Indian carnelian grows redder on exposure to the sun. It is readily available in the form of small polished tumblestones.

History: As far back as 3000 BCE, carnelian and other gemstones were used in Mesopotamia and Egypt as amulets for protection. Carnelian was also reputed to be used as one of the twelve sacred stones set in the breastplate of Aaron. In the Middle Ages, powdered carnelian mixed with water was taken as a remedy against the plague. In medieval times, gemstones were often identified with different emotional states, and carnelian was seen as a healer of anger.

Carnelian stones have a deep warm colour. They also have an attractive mellow sheen.

Healing uses: Carnelian helps to ease depression and gives you a sense of inner stability. It can also help to balance the mind when you are trying to tackle difficult mental tasks. Carnelian warms and stimulates the appetite and balances the female reproductive system, easing menstrual pain. It promotes a sense of attunement with oneself. Its energy is warm, joyful and opening, particularly when it is placed on the lower abdominal area.

Carnelian was a popular healing gem in medieval times. It was used as a remedy against the plague.

Yellow

Yellow is a bright colour that is stimulating to the mind; a positive radiance full of energy and zest. Yellow gemstones sparkle against the skin like sunlight.

Citrine

Geology: Natural citrine is a pale yellow quartz with a gentle sparkle and sheen. True citrine tends to be light in colour. Darker yellow or orange examples may occur naturally or might have been artificially heat-treated. Such stones can often be detected by their reddish sheen. It is possible to obtain very large pieces of citrine as well as delicate crystal clusters and the six-sided terminations that are typical of quartz crystals in general.

Sources: Today most citrine is mined in Brazil in the state of Rio Grande do Sul. Some deposits also exist in Madagascar.

History: The name citrine derives from the French word *citron* (lemon), alluding to the pale yellow colour. In the past, the stone was thought to protect against the venom of poisonous snakes.

The mineral citrine is a beautiful stone to place in your environment.

Healing uses: Citrine clears your mind of conflicting thoughts and provides space to think. It is used to detoxify the body and has a beneficial effect on the kidneys, liver and gall bladder. It tones the digestion and the circulation. It attracts abundance into your life, whether in the form of money or relationships. Try placing it beside your bed to help you sleep.

Carry a piece of citrine with you to keep your mind clear. Yellow is a positive colour to wear as well.

The ancient Egyptians associated yellow topaz with Ra, the sun god. In this wall painting, Ra is the figure sitting in the boat flanked by two baboons.

Topaz has a very effective cleansing effect on the body when it is used in healing.

Topaz

Geology: Topaz is a yellow gemstone that has been used for jewellery for centuries. It is mostly yellow in colour, but it can also be found in orange, red, blue and even green shades. It can form massive clusters of up to a hundred kilograms in weight and is one of the hardest minerals in nature. Its colour has often caused it to be confused with the less valuable citrine, yet it has a beautiful transparent lustre all of its own.

Sources: Brazil is known for high-quality yellow topaz, with other deposits occurring in Sri Lanka, Myanmar and the USA. Russian topaz is pale blue in colour.

History: Ancient Egyptians associated the yellow gemstone with Ra, the sun god, and the Romans with Jupiter, the king of the gods. It was used in protective amulets. A gem thought to have many mystical properties, topaz was said to change colour in the presence of poisons in food or drink – it was even used to detect these. A stunning giant topaz is set in the Portuguese royal crown.

Healing uses: Yellow topaz is useful for focusing your mind on complex problems and generating fresh new ideas. Topaz is valued in healing as a detoxifying stone. It has particularly beneficial effects on the liver, gall bladder and the whole body in general. Topaz also has a toning effect on the nervous system. It helps to enhance overall energy levels and brings inspiration and creativity.

Light Green

Light green is a gentle shade like new golden-green leaves in springtime. It is a youthful energy, fresh and subtle.

Peridot

Geology: Peridot is a variety of olivine, with a lovely pale-green colour provided by iron, nickel and chromium. It is a volcanic gem. In Hawaii on the island of Oahu, you can find volcanic olivine grains on the beaches. Peridot has also been found in meteorite deposits.

Peridot is said to have been a favourite stone of Queen Cleopatra, who must have appreciated its pale green colour.

Sources: More than 3500 years ago, the Egyptians used a peridot from a mine on an island called Zeberget in the Red Sea. This continued to yield gems until after the First World War. Today, most peridot is mined in Arizona, with specimens also found in Myanmar, Brazil and Hawaii. In the 1990s a new deposit was discovered in the Pakistan-owned region of Kashmir.

Peridot stones have a gentle fresh green colour, which is very lightening to the mind and spirit. It is used in healing to reduce stress and tension.

History: Legend has it that peridot was a favourite gemstone of Queen Cleopatra. Peridot is found decorating many medieval churches, including the Shrine of the Three Kings in Cologne Cathedral in Germany. Set in gold, the stone was traditionally credited with the power to drive away evil spirits. Some stones were large enough to be carved into drinking goblets.

Healing uses: Peridot has a light, revitalising effect on your mind and reawakens your appreciation of beauty. It is used in healing to revitalise the heart, spleen and adrenal glands, toning the body and mind, reducing stress and tension. It activates a sense of joy within you.

Jade

Geology: Jade is the name applied to two ornamental stones from China and Central America, nephrite and jadeite. These are very similar in structure and used in similar ways. Jade is a beautiful stone mostly found in various shades of pale to vivid green. Jade is usually cut into smooth dome shapes called cabochons, as well as carved into bangles, beads and statues. Dealers have to gamble when buying jade. They purchase a boulder with only a tiny opening visible from the outside. On splitting, the interior may be found to reveal fine stone or be worthless.

Jade occurs in soft and beautiful shades of green. It looks particularly lovely when carved into statues.

became popular in Europe in the sixteenth century when beautiful artefacts began to be brought over from Central America.

Healing uses: Jade helps to balance emotional states, particularly in highly sensitive individuals. It can calm the heart and soothe away anxiety. Jade is often used in healing to bring the energy of unconditional love and peace into the heart, as well as nurturing and caring for the spirit.

Sources: Top quality jade (jadeite) now comes mostly from Myanmar and Guatemala. The main deposits of nephrite are found in Canada, Australia, the USA and Taiwan.

History: Jade has been the royal gemstone of China for more than 4000 years. Priceless jade artefacts were placed in the tombs of emperors as a symbol of their power and wealth. In Central America, jade was sacred to the Olmec, Mayan and Toltec peoples, who carved it into masks and sacred relics. Jade

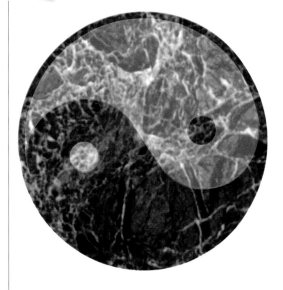

The energy of jade is balancing and harmonising, as suggested by this yin and yang symbol.

Rich Green

Vivid shades of green are soothing to the eye, restful and calming. Green blends yellow and blue, balancing warm and cool energies. Green stones are very beneficial to the heart chakra.

Emerald

Darker green shades are very calming – they are particularly useful when working with the heart chakra.

Geology: Emerald is the green variety of beryl. Its colour is caused by chromium and iron. True emeralds contain tiny inclusions and other flaws. Because emeralds grow in metamorphic layers of rock under pressure, the size of the gems is usually small, with larger examples being very rare.

Sources: Colombia, the producer of the astonishing emeralds associated with the Aztec empire, is still the main producer of fine stones today. Zambia and Brazil also produce top-quality emeralds, as do Zimbabwe, Pakistan and Madagascar.

History: The Aztecs yielded up treasure to the conqueror Hernán Cortes, notably emeralds carved into fish and flowers, with some examples the size of a fist. The colour of the stone made it particularly sacred to the ancient peoples of South America. Emeralds were also found in ancient Egypt – Cleopatra had her own mines near the Red Sea.

Healing uses: The energy of emerald can help to connect you with your creative source. The green colour links you to Nature. In healing, emerald is used to balance the heart and open it up to divine love.

True emeralds have a dramatic effect when set in jewellery. Here they are partnered with gold in a pair of stunning earrings.

Moldavite

Geology: Moldavite is a dark-green form of tektite, which is a kind of fused glass formed when meteor showers hit the Earth millions of years ago. Moldavite is not crystalline in structure; it has swirls, bobbles and craters and forms unusual shapes due to its molten origin. Black and brown tektites exist, but rare dark-green moldavite is the most collectable.

Sources: Moldavia in Eastern Europe is considered to be the best source of green tektite. Fine examples are also found in Moldau in former Czechoslovakia, Thailand and South East Asia, Australia and the USA.

Moldavite falls to Earth from space in meteor showers. Meteorites containing moldavite fuse with geological deposits on the Earth.

Moldavite specimens exist in a range of unusual shapes and sizes.

History: Moldavite is fascinating because of its extraterrestrial origin. It is a fusion of elements from space with geological deposits on the surface of the Earth. It has sometimes been used for making jewellery.

Healing uses: Moldavite can be used to help connect you to deeper levels of spiritual awareness, from the earthly to other dimensions and realms of being. The stone reminds us that we are all travellers through space – even as we go about our daily lives. Our planet is sailing on a continual journey. In healing, the stone can be placed on the forehead to enhance spiritual awareness of our place in the cosmos.

Turquoise

This shade is a fusion of green and blue, a cool and soothing balm to the heart and the emotions. Turquoise stones show up particularly well against darker skins.

Turquoise

Geology: Turquoise is a valuable mineral known scientifically as hydrated copper aluminium phosphate. Its colour ranges from sky blue to various shades of blue-green; the more iron is present, the greener the shade. True specimens contain tiny crystalline deposits that can be seen only with a microscope. There are many fake turquoises on the market that have been stained or dyed. True turquoise is very porous and should not be cleaned with chemicals, just warm soapy water.

Sources: Iran produces very pale sky-blue turquoise with no green tinges and veins; Arizona and New Mexico also yield fine examples. Afghanistan and the Middle East are other sources of the mineral.

Fine turquoise jewellery is still made by talented Navajo craftspeople. The stone looks stunning when set in silver.

History: For thousands of years, Persia was the main source of turquoise. At Sinai in Egypt turquoise was being mined over 5000 years ago. In Mexico, turquoise was revered as a stone fit only for the gods. In the south-west USA, the Native American Navajo continue to make fine turquoise jewellery set in silver.

Healing uses: Turquoise ignites courage in your heart and strengthens your awareness of all life forms. It is used in healing to tone the whole body, as well as easing the lungs, chest and throat and boosting the immune system.

Turquoise is a protective stone that benefits and tones the whole of the immune system.

Aquamarine

Geology: Aquamarine is another variety of beryl, with a pale blue-green colour like sea water – the meaning of its name. The purer the blue shade, the more expensive the stone.

Aquamarine is a popular stone and is most commonly set in silver. This shows off its delicate colour to perfection.

Aquamarine forms hexagonal crystals and is found in coarse granite rocks. Some aquamarines are heat-treated to increase the blue colour. The rough stones have a similar appearance to tourmaline.

Sources: Brazil is the leading producer of aquamarine, with the USA, Zambia, Mozambique and Pakistan also yielding wonderful specimens.

History: Perhaps not surprisingly, there is a great deal of sea folklore and legends associated with aquamarine. It was said to be treasured by mermaids, and was carried by sailors to ensure their safety while at sea. The stone was also seen as a traditional guardian of marriage and it remains an appropriate token to give as an anniversary gift.

Healing uses: Aquamarine expands and uplifts your spirits and helps you think clearly. It is seen as enhancing self-expression and self-worth, particularly in the sphere of your chosen line of work. It has a gently purifying effect on the mind and body, particularly helping the energies of the thyroid, spleen, liver and kidneys. In healing, aquamarine can be placed on the throat to balance the emotions and aid their clear verbal expression. Meditation with aquamarine can help to instil peace and calm in you.

Aquamarine is used to ease the throat in healing work. This aids clear verbal expression and enables the patient to communicate.

Pale Blue

Pale blue is very gentle and soothing to the nerves, the sight and the emotions. Pale-blue stones emit a soft healing energy, which is very much needed in our mad, overexcited world.

Celestite

Geology: Celestite is a form of strontium sulphate. It is a clear transparent mineral with a very pale blue colour deepening to blue-grey, a shade that is unique in the mineral kingdom. It forms larger clusters with pronounced bladed crystals, as well as smaller nodules with tiny inward-growing crystals.

The soft grey-blue of celestite can be used in your environment to soothe and calm the emotions.

Sources: The most abundant sources of celestite tend to be found in sedimentary rocks in the USA, particularly in New York, Michigan and Ohio. Specimens also occur in Germany, Madagascar and Sicily.

Celestite is also known as the stone of heaven, symbolising the sacred energy of angels and celestial beings.

History: Celestite is highly valued among mineral collectors, and over the past few years has become more prominent in New Age shops because of its healing uses.

Healing uses: Celestite is the blue of a summer sky. It brings about expansion, open-heartedness and room to breathe. Placed in a room, celestite calms the energy and is a wonderful focus for meditation. Some healers see it as a stone that symbolises sacred personal space. In healing, it is used to enhance thyroid balance and reduce stress. If placed on the throat, it aids self-expression. It is also useful for healers to use on themselves to replenish their energies.

Blue Moonstone

The changing light of the moon is reflected in the soft lustre of moonstone.

Blue moonstone has a special gentle sheen. No wonder it is considered a sacred stone!

Geology: Moonstone is a member of the feldspar family of minerals. It is a colourless or pale milky stone and when turned in the light, it shows a shimmering translucent blue sheen. This can be a silvery milky white in some specimens, but the blue stones are seen as more valuable. The stone contains layers that reflect light back at each other, creating the shimmering coloured effect. The most effective way of enhancing this property is to cut and polish the stones into cabochons, so they are smooth, rounded domes.

Sources: Some of the best examples of moonstone are to be found in Madagascar, Sri Lanka, Australia, Brazil and the USA.

History: In India, moonstone is considered sacred and is dedicated to the goddess in her lunar forms.

Healing uses: Moonstone is associated with feminine energy and the cyclical nature of feminine rhythms. It brings balance and harmony to your emotions. It is a wonderful stone to mark changing feminine cycles through girlhood to puberty, motherhood and wise-womanhood. It is seen as hormone-balancing and brings equilibrium to the senses. Worn as jewellery set in silver, it is one of the most attractive of the semi-precious stones.

Dark Blue

Rich dark-blue shades are cool and contemplative, bringing a meditative state of calm to the spirit. Deep blue stones are often associated with loyalty and high ideals.

Sapphire

Geology: Sapphire is a variety of corundum, which is the second-hardest known mineral, in the same family as ruby. Mostly known as a source of rich blue stones, sapphire can also be found in other shades like pink, gold, white or even black. Star sapphires contain needles of rutile that reflect a six-pointed star in bright light. Most sapphires have been heat-treated to deepen the colour. Generally sapphires are cut in oval or rounded rectangular forms to display their blue hues.

Sources: Historically, Myanmar and Kashmir are the most famous sapphire producers. However, Sri Lanka produces most of the stones found today, ranging from pale sky-blue to rich, deep shades.

Sapphires have been cut and set in fine jewellery for hundreds of years. Here, diamonds set off an amazing large stone.

Deep blue sapphire is a very 'royal' shade of blue. It is a favourite stone for engagement rings.

History: Traditionally, sapphire was seen as a symbol of fidelity, making it a favourite for engagement rings. It also has an extensive history as a jewel of royalty and high priesthood. The British Crown Jewels contain very large sapphires of 'royal' blue.

Healing uses: Blue sapphire connects you to your highest ideals and spiritual essence. It enables you to communicate your own inner truth. Allow the colour to guide you to your own path of awareness. In healing, sapphire may be applied to the forehead to bring emotional balance and guide your thoughts to the present moment. Sapphire is also said to strengthen the kidneys and the heart.

Lapis Lazuli

Geology: Lapis lazuli is made up of the blue mineral lazurite with golden strands or microcrystals of pyrite and white calcite. The colour of lapis lazuli is always deep blue, and the pyrite crystals help to distinguish it from its cousin sodalite, which is also blue but lacks the pyrite. Lapis tends to be opaque in character. It is porous and should be cleaned only with warm soapy water. It is also fairly brittle and needs careful storage.

Lapis lazuli is a deep blue stone with gold and white strands running through it.

Sources: Lapis lazuli has been mined for over **6000** years. Afghanistan is an ancient source still used today. Lapis is also mined in Chile, the USA, Siberia and Myanmar.

History: The tomb of Tutankhamun yielded up many astonishing treasures, most notably the famous mask of the young king fashioned in gold and lapis lazuli. The Pharaohs were adorned with the stone in life and death. In medieval and Renaissance paintings, enamelling and stained glass, particularly rich shades of blue were obtained by using lapis lazuli ground to a powder.

Healing uses: Lapis lazuli assists with spiritual purification, turning the mind away from earthly concerns. It links you to your higher guidance and opens your inner awareness. With its golden pyrite inclusions, it activates the fire of spiritual illumination, especially if placed on the forehead over the third eye. It is said to bring strength and vitality to the whole body.

Superb jewellery and gold funeral masks inlaid with lapis adorned the body of the young boy king Tutankhamun.

Violet

Purple and violet shades are beneficially stimulating to the brain – as a mixture of energising red and cooling blue, they bring wisdom into action.

Amethyst

Geology: Amethyst is purple quartz that can occur in many forms, ranging from tiny crystals to points, clusters and geodes, which are rocks with inner cavities of varying sizes where the crystals grow inwards. Large geodes are sometimes displayed cut open to show the amethyst formations. Amethyst varies in colour from dark purple to paler lavender shades.

Small amethyst tumblestones are easy to carry with you when you need them.

Sources: Amethyst is found in Brazil, Uruguay, Bolivia and Argentina, Namibia, Zambia and other African countries. The Ural Mountains in Russia produce very fine amethysts cut for jewellery.

History: The Russian monarch Catherine the Great was passionate about amethysts, and there are also many examples found in the British Crown Jewels. Bishops

If you meditate with amethyst, the energy of the stone can clear the whole body.

traditionally wear amethyst rings. The stone has long had a religious connection and it is found decorating many churches and cathedrals.

Healing uses: Amethyst is one of the most popular stones for healing. It will help you to feel spiritually open and aware, purifying and cleansing your energies on physical, mental, emotional and spiritual levels. Placed either on the forehead or above the crown of the head, amethyst energy feels like a shower of cool gentle rain through the whole body. Amethyst can also be used to shield you from negativity.

Iolite

Geology: Iolite is a violet variety of the mineral cordierite, which can also be found in brown or black shades. In the past, iolite was sometimes known as water sapphire because of its beautiful violet-blue hues. It makes very attractive jewellery. Its structure creates a display called pleochroism, where reflections of violet, clear and golden lights appear from different angles within the same stone, making a shimmering effect.

Sources: Iolite deposits are found in many parts of the world, including Sri Lanka, India, Mozambique, Madagascar, Brazil and Myanmar.

History: The Vikings obtained iolite from sources in Norway and Greenland and used thin pieces of the stone as lenses to look up at the sun so they could navigate successfully. The name iolite comes from *ios*, the Greek word for violet.

Iolite shimmers with its own special reflections. It makes really stunning jewellery.

Healing uses: Iolite can be used to focus your meditation on higher dimensions of spirituality. As human beings, we have the capacity to connect with much wider energies than we are aware of in our everyday life. Awareness of our true spiritual home can help us to behave more responsibly and caringly in the physical world. Iolite can be placed above the crown of the head when lying down to meditate or to receive healing. Iolite is also used when trying to balance the energies of the physical body.

The Vikings used iolite that was found in Norway and Greenland.

White

White is a combination of all the colours in the spectrum. Rays of sunlight passing through cut diamonds cause a brilliant rainbow effect. Colourless gems represent unity and perfection.

Diamond

Geology: Diamonds are forever – made of pure carbon, they are the hardest known substance on the Earth, have the highest melting point and atoms packed more densely than any other mineral. Though they are well known as jewellery, diamonds are also used in industry as excellent electrical insulators. Despite their hardness, they have to be handled very skilfully by jewellers because they will split if they are wrongly struck. They occur in clear, pink, pale yellow, blue, green, reddish and even black specimens. Diamonds form in pipelike gaps in a host rock called kimberlite.

Exquisitely cut diamonds reflect all the colours of the spectrum.

Sources: Diamonds are found in South Africa, India, Brazil, Russia, Australia and the USA.

History: There are many famous diamond stories. When the world's largest diamond, the 3106-carat Cullinan was discovered in 1905, workers were seen to play with it like a lump of glass at the edge of a mine shaft in South Africa. The Cullinan was presented to King Edward VII on his sixty-sixth birthday and was cut up into four diamonds that now form part of the British Crown Jewels.

Healing uses: Diamond brings out your unique qualities. This aspect is at the root of its use in rings to mark engagements and long marriages. It is a master healer, activating the purest energy all around and within.

The energy of diamonds is said to bring out your own unique personality.

Clear Quartz

Geology: Quartz is one of the most common minerals found in the Earth's crust. It is found in countless varieties of clusters, points, masses, colours and forms. Clear quartz is also known as rock crystal. Though the stone may be cloudy white, the best quality points are completely clear with an icelike appearance. These stones are well defined, and may be single- or double-terminated. Clear quartz with tiny golden needles of rutile is also called rutilated quartz.

Sources: Brazil, the USA and Africa are among the main sources of the better quality clear quartz.

History: The original meaning of the word 'crystal', usually applied to quartz, is from the Greek word for frozen. Clear quartz is the original crystal ball, with its patterns and milky inclusions providing inspiration for seers. In South America and other locations around the world, large lumps of clear quartz have been found carved into the shape of crystal skulls by ancient peoples.

Fine quartz clusters form in a huge variety of shapes and sizes.

Healing uses: Clear quartz is one of the most commonly used stones in healing. It help to focus and amplify physical, mental and emotional energy. Quartz points can be placed on any areas of the body that need energising. Quartz can also be used protectively in challenging environments. Rutilated quartz eases depression and clears negativity.

Quartz crystals are shown here growing into the available space. Stones like these are often cut in half and polished.

Black

Black absorbs all colours within it, like the rainbow sheen of a starling's wing feathers. Black simply holds all the colours of the spectrum in density. Rather than being negative, black stones have mystery in their depths.

Obsidian

Snowflake obsidian is a particularly attractive version of the usual black obsidian.

Geology: Obsidian is a glassy-textured silicon dioxide, formed from rapidly cooled volcanic lava. Iron and magnesium give the stone its black or very dark green colour. Bubbles of long-trapped air may create rainbow or golden reflections. A particularly attractive form of the stone is snowflake obsidian, which contains white speckled inclusions of cristobalite.

Sources: Obsidian is found in many states of the USA, such as Arizona, Colorado and Texas, as well as in Mexico, Italy and Scotland.

History: Another name for obsidian is 'Apache tear', showing its links to the Native American tribes of the south-western USA. There have been notable archaeological finds of ancient arrow heads chipped from obsidian, indicating its use in hunting and the tooling of leather for at least 10,000 years.

Healing uses: Obsidian has a strong masculine affinity. It affects the energies of the lower abdomen and the root chakra. Meditating with obsidian activates warrior energy when you face uncertainty. It is a very grounding stone, helping to prepare for action, and is said to disperse fear.

This stone turtle, with the white speckled inclusions of cristobalite, is an example of snowflake obsidian.

Native Americans have been hunting with obsidian-tipped arrows for thousands of years.

Black Tourmaline

Geology: The long rectangular shapes of tourmaline and its varied colours make it one of the most popular stones to collect. It occurs in a range of colours, including black, pink, green and blue, as well as forms with more than one colour, such as 'watermelon' with pink inside and green outside. Black tourmaline is called schorl and is the most common opaque form of the stone, very rich in iron. An unusual property of tourmaline is that it can be electrically charged by heating, so one end is positive and the other negative, giving it a kind of magnetic pull. The stone is cut and set in jewellery, carved into figurines and sometimes mounted in uncut form.

Black tourmaline forms into regular shapes and is very popular to collect.

Sources: Kenya, Madagascar and other African countries produce the stone, as well as Brazil, Sri Lanka, Pakistan and the USA.

History: The many colours of tourmaline have made it a favourite with jewel collectors for centuries – the name comes from an old Sinhalese word *turmali*, which means 'mixed'.

The power of a lightning charge crackles through the air. Tourmaline can be electrically charged by heating.

Healing uses: Black tourmaline has a powerful, dense energy that helps to anchor you if you feel unfocused or pulled in different directions. It has a strong protective influence, which can help you when you are emotionally or physically vulnerable. It strengthens and vitalises you and makes you aware of the electromagnetic energies of the Earth. It can be placed on the base of the spine to help stabilise and 'root' your energies.

Brown

Brown is the colour associated with earth, the soil, the dense matter from which all growing things take root; it has a comforting and centring energy. Brown stones are regarded as 'earthing' in healing work.

Smoky Quartz

Smoky quartz occurs in tawny shades of soft brown. It is a very hard mineral.

Geology: Smoky quartz is the brown or black variety of quartz, which is thought to have undergone exposure to radiation during its formation. Smoky quartz is often found in granite rocks that still show a tiny amount of natural radioactivity. Most smoky quartz has been heat-treated to deepen the colour even further. It is often carved into spheres, pyramids, eggs and figurines. Smoky quartz forms well-defined six-sided points and is a mineral as hard as clear quartz. Some specimens also contain golden needles of rutile.

All brown crystals remind us that we come from the Earth, and have a positive grounding effect on the body.

Sources: The world's largest supplier of smoky quartz is Brazil, with the Cairngorm Mountains in Scotland, Colorado in the USA and the Swiss Alps also producing fine specimens.

History: Brown stones like smoky quartz were popular in jewellery in the 1920s and 1930s, particularly in brooches and pendants of neo-Celtic designs.

Healing uses: Smoky quartz helps to strengthen and ground your energies and clear away negativity. Meditation with the stone helps to transform turbulent emotions. It can help to build sexual vitality when used on the lower abdomen and the base of the spine. If you work on a computer, smoky quartz protects against electromagnetic radiation – place a piece on top of your monitor.

Tiger's Eye

Geology: Tiger's eye is a variety of chalcedony, which is quartz containing tiny microcrystals. It is made up of lustrous brown and yellow fibres in layers that reflect the light in an unusual way, causing a phenomenon called 'chatoyancy' (like a cat's eye) when the stone is moved from side to side. It is normally found in shades of brown and gold. However, blue varieties also exist and some heat-treated specimens may have a reddish tinge. Tiger's eye is very attractive when cut and polished in cabochons, smooth rounded shapes that demonstrate the chatoyancy more clearly.

Because of its fibres, tiger's eye shimmers with a luminous glow. This looks best when it is carved into cabochon shapes.

Sources: Large deposits are found in Myanmar, India, Australia and South Africa.

History: In medieval times, tiger's eye was often used as a protection against the evil eye.

Healing uses: With a combination of earthy brown and radiant gold shades, tiger's eye is useful to help spirit into matter, bringing ideas into reality. When you embark on a new path of expansion, it stabilises you and makes sure you that have your feet on the ground. It is thought to be a relaxing and calming stone, which can be helpful for inducing sleep. Used over the solar plexus or the abdomen, it helps to balance and harmonise both physical and emotional energies.

Use tiger's eye to relax and calm your mind. It is a stone with very calming energies.

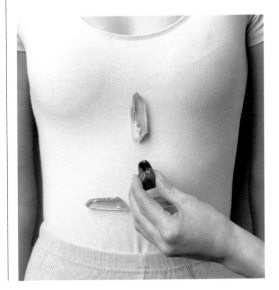

Iridescent

Iridescence is not so much a colour as a quality, a sudden appearance of shimmering colours as light moves over a surface. Iridescent stones have long been regarded as having magical properties.

Labradorite

Geology: The beautiful mineral labradorite may show iridescent flashes in a whole variety of shades across its surface – deep blue, violet, green, gold and orange. It is quite dull in appearance until light plays upon it in the right direction. The effect is caused by different intergrowing layers in its structure, which reflect light waves back against each other, creating the play of colours. Labradorite with many thin layers will show the best effects. As a mineral, it is a variety of feldspar, and forms in chunks embedded in host rocks.

Sources: It is mostly found in Labrador, Canada – from where it gets its name – and also in Scandinavia, where it is sold under the name 'spectrolite'. Some deposits occur in the USA and Russia.

History: The beautiful variety of colours and changing appearance of labradorite have caused it to be used as a magical talisman since ancient times.

Healing uses: Labradorite reminds you of the changing nature of life moment by moment. Flashes of deep blue within the stone help you to recall that spirit is behind and within all matter. Labradorite expands the third eye and the crown, opening you up to deeper perceptions of reality, and encouraging you to see with new eyes. Its gently shimmering colours may also help to bring you interesting dreams.

Shimmering labradorite displays many hues. It can bring you vivid dreams and enable you to see beyond reality.

Opal

Geology: Opals are not true crystals. Classed as mineraloids, they have a unique structure. They formed millions of years ago as a solution that settled in the cracks and layers of sedimentary rocks, and opals still contain between 6 and 10 per cent water. Packed with minuscule spheres of silicon and oxygen molecules, opals flash with many tiny shimmering rainbows as light bounces in these microscopic spaces – the effect is known as 'opalescence'. The stone's background may be clear, milky white, pale yellow, black or even the orange-red that is found in fire opals. Black opals contain the brightest colours and are also the most expensive.

Sources: Ancient opal came from mines in Eastern Europe, but for the past one hundred years the main producer has been Australia. Fire opals are found in Mexico and in the state of Oregon in the USA.

History: Few stones have had such a varied and fascinating history as opals. There have been many archaeological finds of opal artefacts that are thousands of years old. Opals were adored by the ancient Romans; used as an eye tonic in the Middle Ages;

Opals look very good in simple jewellery settings and look particularly attractive when they are set in rings.

celebrated by Shakespeare; and were a favourite gemstone of Queen Victoria.

Healing uses: Opal is alive with gentle shimmers of iridescent colour. The most common background is a milky white. This makes the stone very much in tune with the third eye and the crown chakras. The stone can be used to enhance psychic awareness as well as energising all levels and areas of the body, because of the rainbow of colours that is contained within it.

Opals shimmer with their own beautiful rainbow colours. They can be used to energise the whole of the body.

Gold

Gold as a colour ray is radiant, and as warm and bright as the sun itself. The precious metal has been treasured as a setting for gemstones and jewels since the beginning of humankind, and gold minerals are strongly attractive.

The Metal Gold

The hues of the metal gold have mesmerised humankind for thousands of years.

Geology: Gold is a rare and noble metal. Its chemical symbol is Au, which comes from *aurum*, the Latin word for gold. Gold is soft enough to be beaten into fine leaves, and 28 grammes can make a gold wire 80 kilometres in length. Its purity is measured in carats, a word derived from Italian, Greek and Arabic words for carob seeds, which were used to balance the scales in ancient trading practices. Pure gold is 24 carat. A combination of yellow gold with copper is often known as red gold, and with platinum, white gold.

Sources: Today, gold is extensively mined in California, Mexico, Colorado and Canada.

History: Examples of gold jewellery date back thousands of years. The art of smelting and working gold produced amazing Egyptian, Sumerian and South American artefacts. It has traditionally been a symbol of nobility and royalty. The would-be conquerors of the New World sought El Dorado, the fabled city made entirely of gold.

Healing uses: Gold is seen as cleansing to the whole body, but particularly to the brain and the nervous system. Wearing gold helps to attract positive energy and abundance. In medicine, gold is used to treat rheumatoid arthritis, ulcers, certain types of cancer and to repair damaged tissues in surgery.

Pure gold in bars is one of the most valuable commodities to be found. It is immediately associated with wealth and power.

Early gold panners often mistook pyrite for gold. Although it looks very similar, pyrite has to be worked in a different way.

Pyrite

Geology: Pyrite is a beautiful mineral with a yellow sheen like brass. It is also known as 'fool's gold' because it has often been mistaken for the real thing. It is very common and forms opaque crystals with precise, geometric, often cuboid formations. It has a high percentage of iron and sulphur in its composition. Pyrite has the same chemistry as marcasite, and the two are difficult to distinguish from each other.

Pyrite is twice as hard as gold and cannot be worked in the same way, although the variety from Italy can be faceted for jewellery.

Sources: Significant quantities of pyrite have been found in the states of Missouri and Illinois, USA. Other sources have also been discovered in South Africa, Peru, Germany, Russia, Italy and Spain.

History: Although the mineral has a high iron content, pyrite has never been used as a source of iron. However, during the Second World War, pyrite was mined as a source of sulphur for industrial purposes. Any jewellery that is labelled as marcasite is in fact more likely to be pyrite, because marcasite slowly deteriorates over time.

Healing uses: Pyrite is seen as an overall cleanser of the body, and if brought into your environment it helps to dispel negativity and clear your electromagnetic field. Place it on your desk when working to improve your energy levels. In healing, pyrite can be placed at the base of the spine or on the lower abdomen to boost your energy.

Pyrite has a different sheen from gold – it is paler and looks more like brass.

Silver

The changing energy of the silver ray is like the moon shining on water, delicate and pure, with a fluidity that is cooling and soothing to the senses. Silver as a metal and silver-grey stones have a subtle sheen against the skin.

°The Metal Silver

Geology: Silver is a metal with the symbol Ag for *argentum*, the Latin word for silver. It can occur alone in nature and is also often found with gold, copper or mercury deposits. It is extremely soft, like gold, and is the most electrically and thermally conductive metal, making it very useful in the photographic, watch-making and computer industries. It can be drawn without breaking into fine wire the thickness of human hair. Fine silver is 999 parts per thousand pure; most jewellery is set in sterling silver, which is 925 parts silver with 75 parts copper.

Red-hot silver ore pours into a waiting mould. Like gold, silver is extremely soft and can be worked very easily.

Sources: Silver is widely distributed all over the globe. The most notable deposits today are situated in Mexico, Canada and in Arizona in the USA.

History: Many examples of stunning silver jewellery and artefacts can be found in ancient Celtic, Roman and Indian civilisations. Silver has often been associated with the moon because of its silvery shimmer.

Healing uses: The energy of silver is cool, as opposed to the bright radiance of gold. Silver is subtle, seen as linked to the unconscious, bringing intuitive impulses. Silver connects you with your dream-self, the part of you that is mysterious and knowing.

The soft silver glow of moonlight encases the Earth in a silver radiance. Silver connects you to this moon energy.

Haematite has an attractive matt sheen to it. It is used to warm and strengthen blood circulation and increase physical energy.

Haematite

Geology: Haematite is iron oxide, a mineral that is a source of opaque, silver-grey crystals. The host rock and its dust are blood-red in colour, providing a natural source of red pigment. Haematite may form crystals in a number of shapes and masses – rounded kidney-shaped stones as well as bladed crystals can be found.

Sources: Notable specimens can be found in the Lake District in Northern England, Mexico, Brazil, Australia and Canada.

History: In ancient times, the red rocks of haematite were said to be formed from the blood of warriors who died in battle. The word 'haematite' comes from the Greek root *haem*, which refers to the blood. Traditionally it was held by women in childbirth. For centuries and even until recently, finely ground particles of red haematite dust were used in make-up formulations as blusher!

Healing uses: Haematite is a grounding and strengthening stone, which helps to centre you very much in the body, particularly when your energies are overstretched. It has a calming and soothing effect on the nerves. It can be worn to strengthen courage and energy when facing difficult challenges. Haematite also counteracts negative energy in your environment, for example, when placed near a computer. In healing, it is considered to balance blood circulation.

Haematite powder is blood red and is therefore used in healing work to treat blood disorders and the circulatory system.

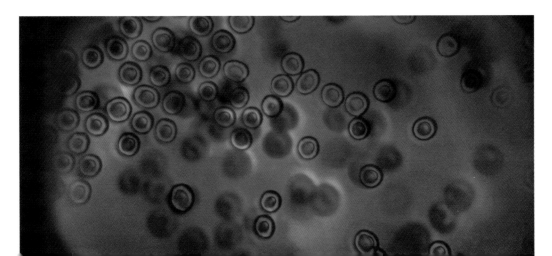

Simple Crystal Healing Methods

Working with crystal energies involves fine-tuning your intuition and sensitivity to your environment. You can use the chart on page 19, or choose a crystal from the Crystal Index because of its colours or associations. Alternatively, you can simply work with a stone because you feel that it is the right one for you.

What is Healing?

The word 'healing' is derived from an old Germanic root *hael*, which can mean 'complete', 'whole' or even 'holy'. It is a process by which the body, mind and spirit are gently balanced to bring a sense of wholeness, oneness with all life. Anyone can benefit from healing, provided they

Crystals can be hung on a chain so that you can use them as pendulums for dowsing work.

Gently laying a crystal over your heart area can soothe any troubled emotions.

are open to receiving it. If you have complex physical problems or deep emotional issues, you are advised to seek the help of a suitably qualified practitioner. For general balancing and opening your own awareness, you can benefit from working on yourself. After any exercises it is useful to make notes or drawings you can come back to at a later date – healing is an ever-unfolding process.

Using a Pendulum

A pendulum can be made of a balanced quartz or cut-glass point suspended on a chain or a string. Dowsing, as this is called, is an ancient art. If you hold the pendulum still and say your real name, it should respond by turning clockwise. If you say a false name, it should swing from side to side or anti-clockwise. With practice, you will get used to how your pendulum shows 'yes' and 'no'. You can then sit and touch each chakra area from base to crown with one hand, asking if that level needs energy, and watching the pendulum swing in response. You can also simply hold the pendulum over a stone and ask if it is the right one to use at this time.

Working with a Single Crystal

Prepare your space: clear away everyday clutter, light a candle and perhaps some incense. Select a suitable stone for yourself – by intuition, dowsing or by consulting the chart or Crystal Index – and sit quietly holding it in your hands. Breathe deeply and relax. Take your awareness into your body and note any tensions. Using your breath, simply dissolve them like clouds in a blue sky. Then take your awareness to your stone – to its colour, shape and feeling in your hands. Relax and see what impressions or feelings come to you for a few minutes. To come out of the process, take a few deep breaths and gently stretch your arms and hands.

Holding a crystal in your hands can help to fine-tune your intuition. What exactly are you expecting from this mineral?

Using Crystals on the Body

Lie down comfortably on a mat on the floor. Place a piece of rose quartz over your heart and then relax, slowly breathing away any tension in your body. Silently and gently focus your intention on opening and expanding the energies in your heart chakra. Breathe into the heart area and visualise the rose quartz crystal shining the light of unconditional love into your whole being. Now visualise that rosy ray expanding beyond you to include all life forms. To end the exercise, take a few slow, deep breaths and then flex your fingers and toes before slowly getting up.

Living With Crystals

Crystals can play a vital part in making your environment beautiful wherever you are. You may choose them for their beauty, or for a particular function that is relevant to you or your living space. Here are some ideas for placing and using crystals in your space.

Bedroom

It is worth saying here that too many crystals in the bedroom may not be such a good idea: you mostly want to relax and sleep in there, so too many amplified energies may not help! Having said that, stones like tiger's eye, amethyst and rose quartz are said to be gentle and restful to have around you, perhaps at your bedside. If you want to enhance the energy for love-making, don't forget Cleopatra's favourite green stones like peridot or the expansive warm energy of amber. In a child's bedroom, a gentle blue stone like celestite brings a sense of peace and calm.

Try placing a crystal on your computer monitor to balance your environment and disperse negative energies.

Study or Office

Here electromagnetic radiation from computers is the main issue. Stones like smoky quartz or amethyst can be used to help maintain a balanced environment. Try placing a stone on top of your monitor. If you are to have a meeting you feel may be challenging, you can place a large piece of rose quartz in the middle of the table to calm the energies. If you need inspiration, a beautiful clear quartz cluster is a wonderful,

Focusing on your chosen crystals can help clear away negativity and generate new ideas. Remember that stones constantly used for this need regular cleansing.

complex, light-filled shape to concentrate on, clearing your mind for new ideas. Stones that sit constantly in an electronic environment will need regular cleansing.

Bathroom

It can be very restful to put little smooth polished crystals in the bath with you. Water is a great conductor, so the bath will be gently energised by them – and so will you. Rose quartz, carnelian, citrine, amethyst or tiger's eye are fun to try. Place the crystals in the bath, run the water, and add three to four drops of an essential oil like lavender or frankincense, light a candle on the window sill and lie back for a lovely mystical soak.

Crystals really come into their own when they are placed in water. Try bathing with crystals in the bath for a really restful soak.

Combine crystals, fresh flowers and candles to create a beautiful and uplifting living space.

Living Room

Here you may wish to create a special space for your crystals. A good idea is to set aside a particular table covered with a silk cloth, with a beautiful candle in a holder, a vase for fresh flowers, and an incense holder, as well as your stones. In India, and other countries, many houses have their own small shrines, which are tended daily. A beautiful arrangement of crystals, candles and fresh flowers is an attractive focal point and helps to provide a wonderful energy in your living room. Even the intrusive presence of a television set can be enhanced by an amethyst cluster placed on it, which helps balance electromagnetic rays as well.

Meditating With Crystals

Meditation is a way of accessing a state of deep stillness, which is health-giving in this fast-moving modern age. In a meditative state, you experience deep peace and relaxation. This allows your body to restore itself on a cellular level, and your mind and spirit to be regenerated.

Meditation aims to create in your mind the stillness and peace that is found in nature. It can be very energising.

Making Time and Creating Space

Meditation is not 'doing nothing', it is allowing yourself time to just 'be', releasing yourself from daily demands for a short and beneficial time. Try to arrange a regular fifteen-minute slot each day for yourself and see how it works for you.

Crystals as a Focus

For meditation, crystals can be contemplated as a fixed object, held in the hands, or placed on the body. To develop the earlier exercises, you can add in visualisation, allowing the power of your creative imagination and intuition to respond to the crystal. After these exercises, try writing notes or drawing your experiences and keep them as a reference.

Clear Quartz Exercise: Inner Cleansing

Using a clear quartz cluster or point, sit holding the crystal in your hands. Breathe deeply and release all tension from your body for a few moments. Now imagine a fountain of white light that begins just above the crown of your head and enters

Sit and relax and allow your creative imagination to run free. If you also hold your crystal you can allow your imagination to work on that too.

Use a crystal that feels right to you at the time. You will know instinctively which one is right for you.

your skull, flowing down your face, neck, back, shoulders, arms, hands and into your crystal. As the energy builds in the crystal, allow it to flow on down your abdomen, hips, legs and into the Earth. Thank the Earth for her gifts. Imagine yourself to be a conduit between Earth and Heaven. To end the exercise, breathe deeply and flex your feet and hands.

your head, up the tree, and out into the universe. Relax and feel yourself to be a part of all Nature. Breathe deeply and stretch your arms to come out of the exercise – and thank the tree for allowing you to do this.

You can work with any stones that seem appropriate to you – with time, you will develop your own favourites. Try to be aware and thankful at all times for the gifts of the mineral kingdom and the Earth.

All stones, minerals and precious gems come from the Earth. Try to remember this at all times.

Amber Exercise: Connecting to the Plant Kingdom

Amber is an organic gemstone made up of fossilised tree resin, often containing tiny pollen grains or other ancient life forms. For this exercise, take a piece of amber with you on a walk. If possible, find a tall pine tree, or if none are nearby, let your intuition guide you to a tree. Stand with your back to the trunk and hold the amber in your hands. Breathe deeply and feel the upright strength of the tree. Imagine you are drawing warm earth energy up though your feet, your legs, hips, abdomen and into the amber in your hands. Allow the energy to continue flowing up through your back, heart, shoulders and up out of

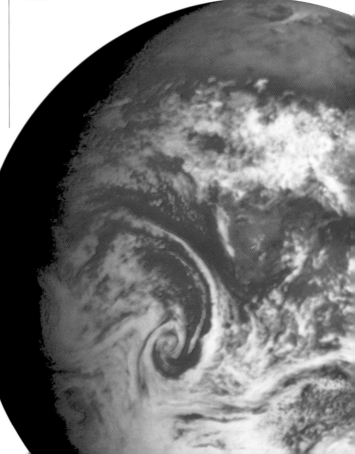

Buying Crystals

Obtaining crystals for your collection can be a lot of fun; however, a little preparation is a good idea. Use these guidelines to help you make informed and appropriate choices so you are happy with your purchases and feel they are right for you.

Buy your crystals from a supplier who will give you helpful advice and important information.

Today crystals are widely available from a variety of sources. You can buy inexpensive stones that are both aesthetically appealing and are useful for healing purposes.

Finding a Supplier

When you are buying crystals, it really helps to do your research. Your local telephone directory may contain listings of crystal shops and outlets. If you know a crystal healing practitioner, ask them where they source their stones – perhaps they will sell to you. The main thing is, visit as many of these people and places as you can. Feel the atmosphere: are the stones housed and displayed with care? If you ask questions (as you should), are you given helpful answers and advice? Many stones on the market are heat-treated, dyed or grown artificially in a laboratory. Ask the supplier where their stones come from. If they are unwilling to discuss it, think twice about buying. Many fairs and trade shows supply crystals, and the same guidelines apply here. Get to know your retailer and trust your intuition. There are mail order crystal companies, but the disadvantage is that you do not see or handle the stones before you buy. Your personal experience of the stones is important, particularly if you want them for healing work.

Try out crystals in the shop and feel which ones are right for you. This is a vital part of buying your stones.

Natural minerals can be collected from beaches or other locations. Be sure that you have permission to do this.

Collecting Crystals

Mineral collecting is a popular hobby. Even collecting stones from the beach or rivers is a fun pastime. Your local museum may know of a geological group who go out collecting, and it is a wonderful experience to see rocks in veins in a natural setting. If you live in a granite area, for example, it will be possible to find stones with small quartz crystals embedded in them. It is best to join a group so that you do not get into trouble for trespassing or for doing any environmental damage.

Buying for Other People

Some crystal healing books suggest you should choose your own stones rather than choose them for other people – again, because of the personal interaction between the holder and the stone. To choose for someone, you really need to ask your intuition, visualise the person and ask if the stone is right for them.

The beauty and variety of crystals means that you will always find something to suit your purpose and your price range.

Birthstone List

This may also help when choosing crystals for other people. Birthstone lists became very popular in the eighteenth and nineteenth centuries and do vary, but here is a general selection.

January	garnet	
February	amethyst	
March	aquamarine	
April	diamond	
May	tourmaline	
June	moonstone	
July	carnelian	
August	peridot	
September	lapis lazuli	
October	opal	
November	topaz	
December	turquoise	

Glossary

Here is a list of terms that occur in the text with explanations.

Cabochon
a gem cut and polished into a smooth, domed shape.

Chakra
the energy centre in the body.

Chatoyancy
a shimmering light-effect like a cat's eye, e.g. in tiger's eye.

Cleansing
the practice of cleaning crystals physically and energetically.

Conductor
an agent that allows the free flow of heat or electricity.

Crystal
a mineral with a precise geometrically arranged structure.

Element
one of the basic building blocks of matter, e.g. carbon or hydrogen.

Face
one of the sides of a crystal.

Geode
a hollow lump of rock with crystals growing inward.

Geology
the science of the history and development of the Earth and its minerals.

Inclusion
specks, bubbles or other minerals showing up in crystals.

Inorganic
a substance of inert origin like a mineral.

Iridescence
a shimmering multicoloured play of light.

Magma
molten rock at the Earth's core.

Mineral
a natural inorganic chemical compound.

Molten
melted or in liquid form, e.g. volcanic lava.

Nodule
a small lump of rock.

Opalescence
a milky, soft, luminous sheen, as in opals.

Organic
a substance with a plant or animal origin.

Programming
conscious intent directed into a crystal for healing purposes.

Rutile
strands of golden mineral appearing in clear quartz and other stones.

Setting
the art of placing gemstones in precious metal.

Termination
the pointed end of a crystal.

Tumblestones
small, smooth, crystal pebbles rounded off in a machine.

Useful Addresses and Websites

The Internet is full of amazing and informative websites on crystals. Here are a few:

The site of the International Colored Gemstone Association

Website: www.gemstone.org

Site for information on British Crown Jewels

Website: www.royal.gov.uk

Useful geological information

Website: www.mineralgalleries.com
Website: www.nationalgeographic.com good for superb photographic material

The Natural History Museum, London, UK

Website: www.nhm.ac.uk

The International Association of Crystal Healing Therapists (IACHT)

publishes a list of accredited therapists in the UK and details of training in crystal healing:
PO Box 344, Manchester, M60 2EZ, UK
www.iacht.co.uk

The Crystalis Institute

set up by Naisha Ahsian in the USA offers courses in crystal healing: 440 Bayley Hazen Road, Walden, Vermont, USA
Website: www.crystalisinstitute.com

The European College of Vibrational Medicine

is an online distance learning college with courses on crystal healing
Website: www.raven.org.uk

Index